This Book Belongs To:

_____

Awesome Picture of Me

BIBLE STUDY NOTES

DATE _____

BOOK

CHAPTER

VERSES

SONGS WE SANG

THE MOST IMPORTANT THING I LEARNED

HOW CAN I USE WHAT I LEARNED

WHAT DID I LEARN ABOUT JESUS

SOMETHING I AM GRATEFUL FOR

DRAW A PICTURE ABOUT TODAY'S LESSON

BIBLE STUDY NOTES

DATE _____

BOOK   CHAPTER   VERSES

WHO OR WHAT WAS THE LESSON ABOUT?

WHAT DOES THIS HAVE TO DO WITH ME?

WHAT HAPPENS?

A PICTURE OF WHAT I AM GRATEFUL FOR

BIBLE STUDY NOTES

DATE _____

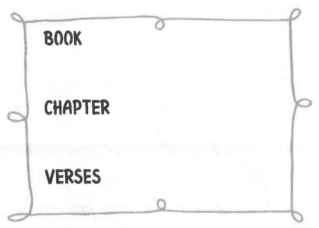

BOOK

CHAPTER

VERSES

TODAY I SANG

DRAW A PICTURE

TODAY I LEARNED

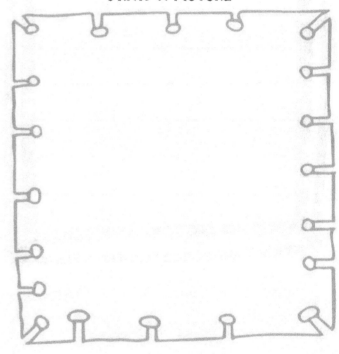

I FEEL GOD'S LOVE FOR ME...

1.

2.

3.

I AM GRATEFUL FOR

_____

_____

AND IT MAKES ME FEEL

GOOD   GREAT   AWESOME

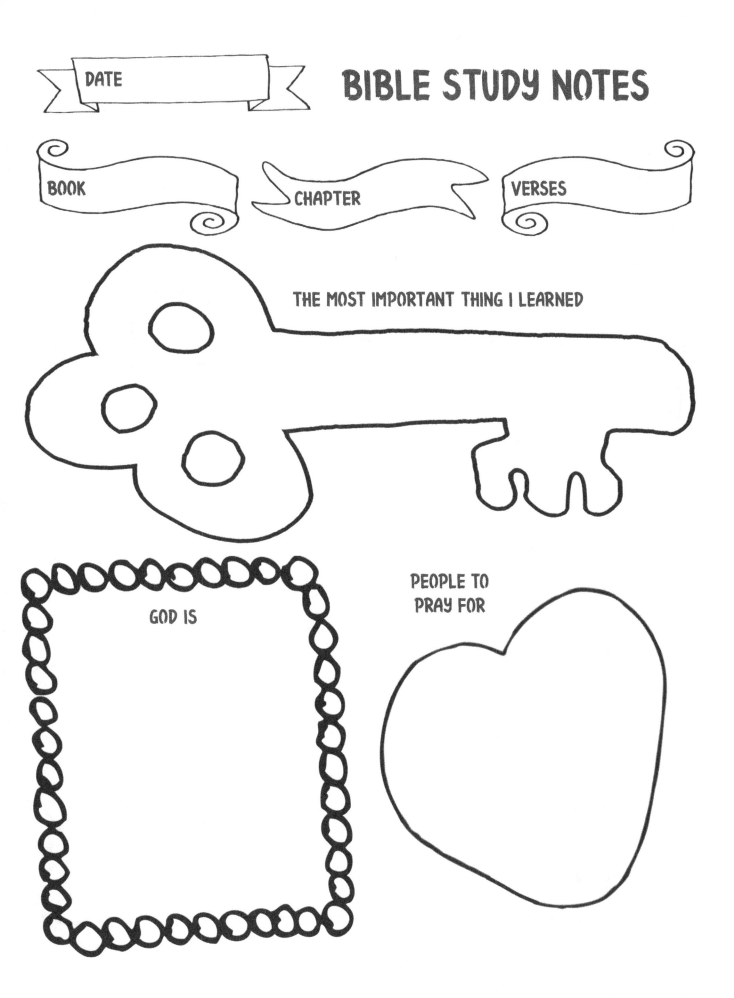

DATE

BIBLE STUDY NOTES

BOOK

CHAPTER

VERSES

THE MOST IMPORTANT THING I LEARNED

GOD IS

PEOPLE TO PRAY FOR

Gratitude
Scavenger Hunt

Find Something I Am Grateful For

1. That makes me happy _____

2. That is soft _____

3. That I love _____

4. That is outside _____

5. That needs sun to grow _____

6. That is warm _____

7. That is shiny _____

8. That is red _____

9. That is wiggly _____

10. That is musical _____

DATE

BIBLE STUDY NOTES

DATE _____

BOOK

CHAPTER

VERSES

SONGS WE SANG

THE MOST IMPORTANT THING I LEARNED

HOW CAN I USE WHAT I LEARNED

WHAT DID I LEARN ABOUT JESUS

SOMETHING I AM GRATEFUL FOR

DRAW A PICTURE ABOUT TODAY'S LESSON

BIBLE STUDY NOTES

DATE _____

BOOK   CHAPTER   VERSES

WHO OR WHAT WAS THE LESSON ABOUT?

_____
_____
_____
_____
_____
_____
_____
_____

WHAT DOES THIS HAVE TO DO WITH ME?

A PICTURE OF WHAT I AM GRATEFUL FOR

WHAT HAPPENS?

_____
_____
_____
_____
_____
_____
_____

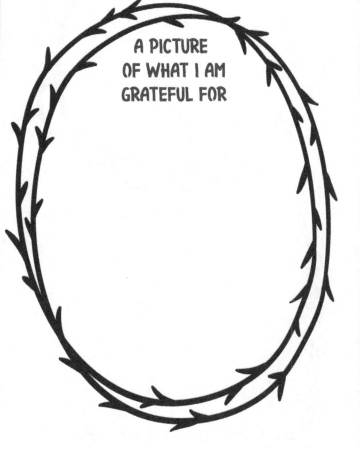

BIBLE STUDY NOTES

DATE _____

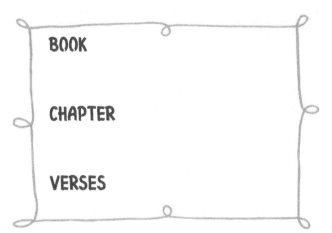

BOOK

CHAPTER

VERSES

TODAY I SANG

DRAW A PICTURE

TODAY I LEARNED

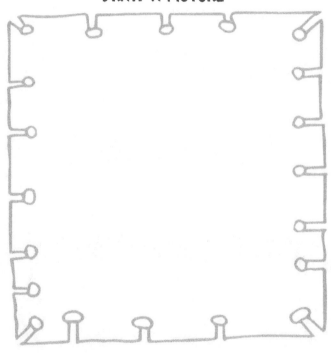

I FEEL GOD'S LOVE FOR ME...

I AM GRATEFUL FOR

_____

_____

AND IT MAKES ME FEEL

GOOD   GREAT   AWESOME

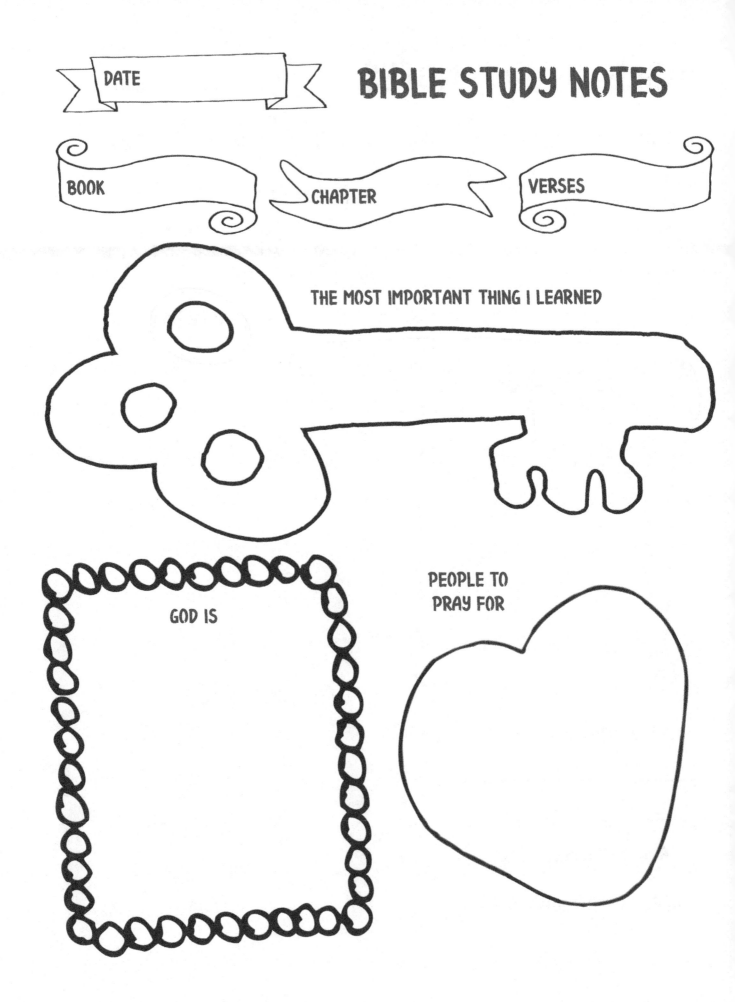

DATE

BIBLE STUDY NOTES

BOOK

CHAPTER

VERSES

THE MOST IMPORTANT THING I LEARNED

GOD IS

PEOPLE TO PRAY FOR

Tell a favorite Bible Story as a Comic Strip

DATE:

BIBLE STUDY NOTES

DATE _____

BOOK

CHAPTER

VERSES

SONGS WE SANG

THE MOST IMPORTANT THING I LEARNED

HOW CAN I USE WHAT I LEARNED

WHAT DID I LEARN ABOUT JESUS

SOMETHING I AM GRATEFUL FOR

DRAW A PICTURE ABOUT TODAY'S LESSON

BIBLE STUDY NOTES

DATE _____

BOOK   CHAPTER   VERSES

WHO OR WHAT WAS THE LESSON ABOUT?

WHAT DOES THIS HAVE TO DO WITH ME?

WHAT HAPPENS?

A PICTURE OF WHAT I AM GRATEFUL FOR

BIBLE STUDY NOTES

DATE _____

BOOK

CHAPTER

VERSES

TODAY I SANG

DRAW A PICTURE

TODAY I LEARNED

I FEEL GOD'S LOVE FOR ME...

I AM GRATEFUL FOR

1.

2.

_____

_____

3.

AND IT MAKES ME FEEL

GOOD   GREAT   AWESOME

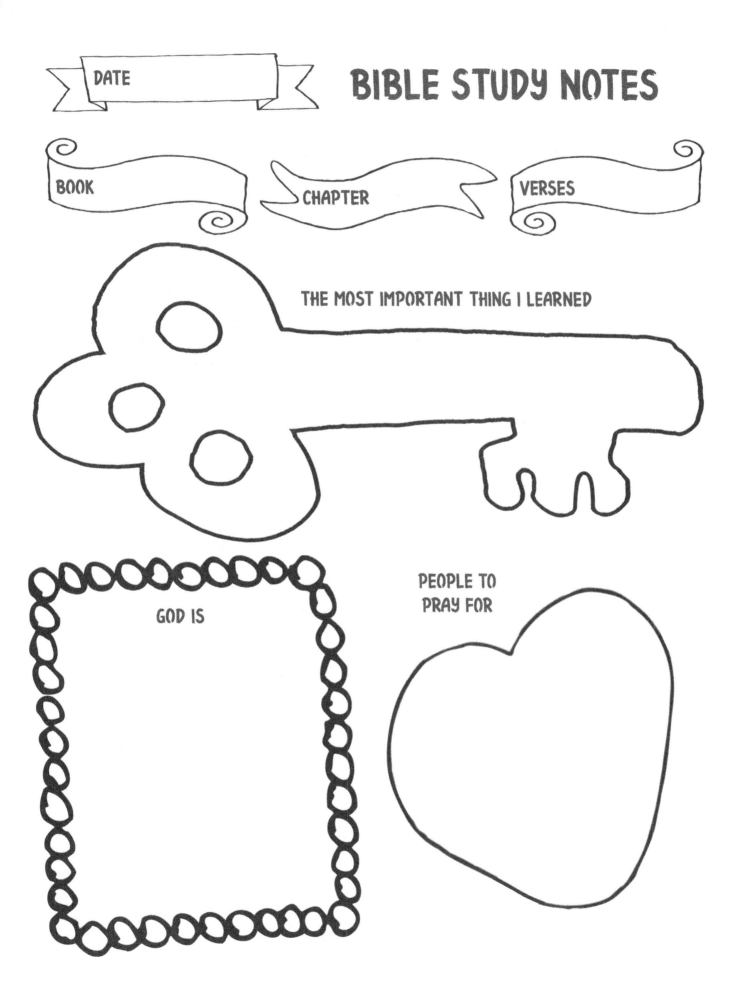

DATE

BIBLE STUDY NOTES

BOOK

CHAPTER

VERSES

THE MOST IMPORTANT THING I LEARNED

GOD IS

PEOPLE TO PRAY FOR

The following words can be found in the diagram below reading forward, backward, up, down and diagonally. Find the words and circle them.

jerusalem   peace
jesus   wrath
jehovah   david
prophecy   blood
cross   gold
lucifer   man

F I F O T Z P C K V K Z P O F L
U O C R P J D Z N A Y N Y E U Y
O K H T Y B T O D D K O D C Z C
I G M T Q L L F U O F I I O D V
N O A I U C S B W R P F D P F G
M L N T P U W P X F E J N R U T
E D L I Z U X D Q R A L L K N E
L M J V P Y B Y W S C R R O G H
A O U P C L C K W X E T V S Q A
S Y I B K E T P O G Y K W X L V
U S P C H K E J Y Z Z B C L J O
R X I P T C T A T S J V R C C H
E K O R A J I B F G N Y O W Q E
J R I A R Z H A Y I S U S E J J
P L I G W U K Z U D R E S Z U H
J L D A V I D Q B L O O D S N W

BIBLE STUDY NOTES

DATE _____

BOOK

CHAPTER

VERSES

SONGS WE SANG

THE MOST IMPORTANT THING I LEARNED

HOW CAN I USE WHAT I LEARNED

WHAT DID I LEARN ABOUT JESUS

SOMETHING I AM GRATEFUL FOR

DRAW A PICTURE ABOUT TODAY'S LESSON

BIBLE STUDY NOTES

DATE _____

BOOK   CHAPTER   VERSES

WHO OR WHAT WAS
THE LESSON ABOUT?

WHAT DOES THIS
HAVE TO DO WITH ME?

A PICTURE
OF WHAT I AM
GRATEFUL FOR

WHAT HAPPENS?

BIBLE STUDY NOTES

DATE _____

TODAY I SANG

BOOK

CHAPTER

VERSES

DRAW A PICTURE

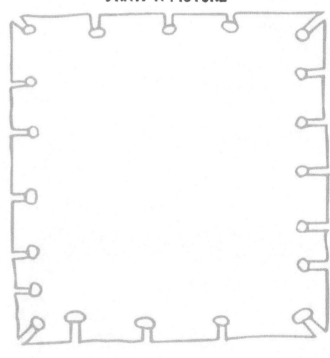

TODAY I LEARNED

I AM GRATEFUL FOR

_____

_____

AND IT MAKES ME FEEL

GOOD   GREAT   AWESOME

I FEEL GOD'S LOVE FOR ME...

1.

2.

3.

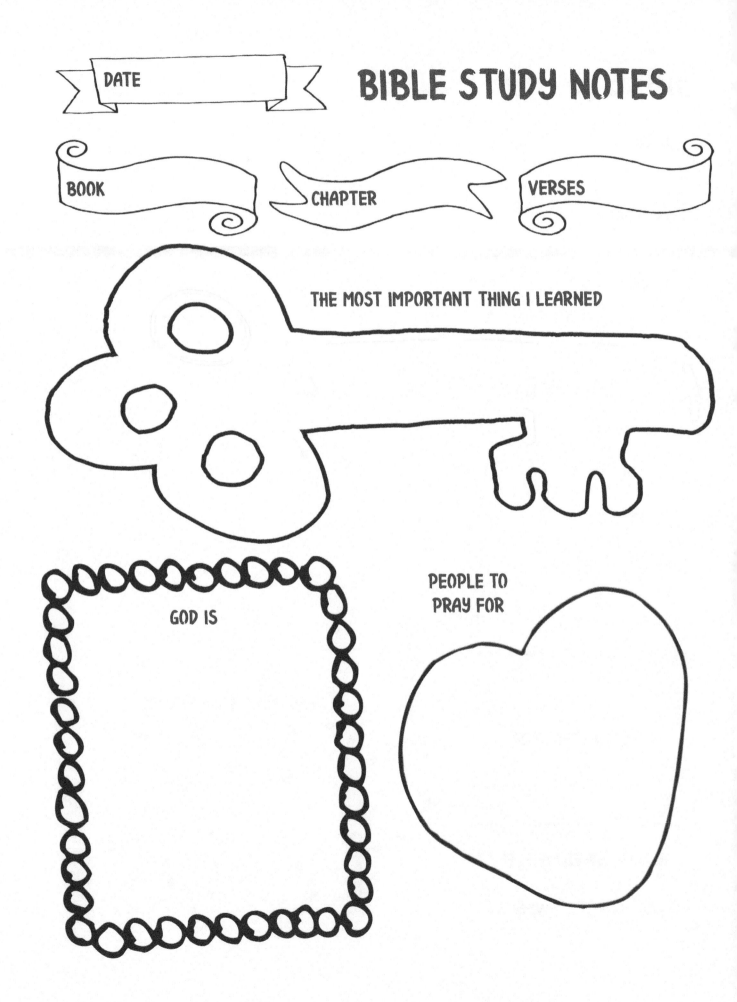

DATE

BIBLE STUDY NOTES

BOOK

CHAPTER

VERSES

THE MOST IMPORTANT THING I LEARNED

GOD IS

PEOPLE TO PRAY FOR

Gratitude
Scavenger Hunt

Find Something I Am Grateful For

1. That makes me smile

_____

2. That is round

_____

3. That sings

_____

4. That is prickly

_____

5. That is blue

_____

6. That glows

_____

7. That is found on grass

_____

8. That is crunchy

_____

9. That tastes sour

_____

10. That is sandy

_____

DATE

BIBLE STUDY NOTES

DATE _____

BOOK

CHAPTER

VERSES

SONGS WE SANG

THE MOST IMPORTANT THING I LEARNED

HOW CAN I USE WHAT I LEARNED

WHAT DID I LEARN ABOUT JESUS

SOMETHING I AM GRATEFUL FOR

DRAW A PICTURE ABOUT TODAY'S LESSON

BIBLE STUDY NOTES

DATE _____

BOOK   CHAPTER   VERSES

WHO OR WHAT WAS THE LESSON ABOUT?

WHAT DOES THIS HAVE TO DO WITH ME?

WHAT HAPPENS?

A PICTURE OF WHAT I AM GRATEFUL FOR

BIBLE STUDY NOTES

DATE _____

BOOK

CHAPTER

VERSES

TODAY I SANG

DRAW A PICTURE

TODAY I LEARNED

I FEEL GOD'S LOVE FOR ME...

1.

2.

3.

I AM GRATEFUL FOR

_____

_____

AND IT MAKES ME FEEL

GOOD   GREAT   AWESOME

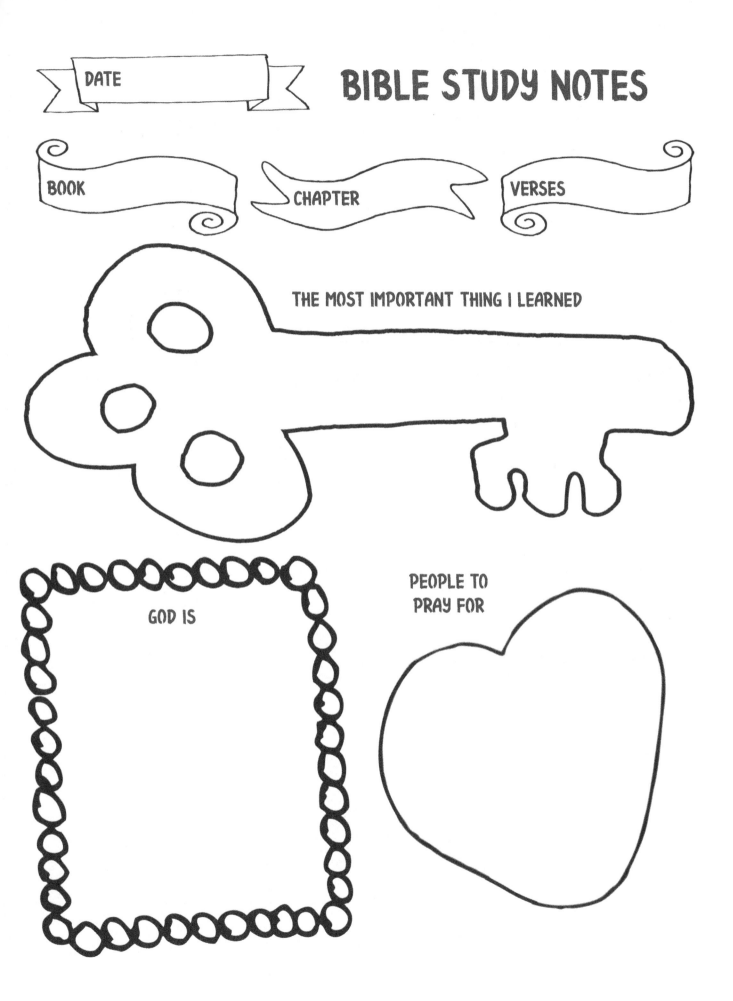

DATE

BIBLE STUDY NOTES

BOOK

CHAPTER

VERSES

THE MOST IMPORTANT THING I LEARNED

GOD IS

PEOPLE TO PRAY FOR

Tell a favorite Bible Story as a Comic Strip

DATE:

BIBLE STUDY NOTES

DATE _____

BOOK

CHAPTER

VERSES

SONGS WE SANG

THE MOST IMPORTANT THING I LEARNED

HOW CAN I USE WHAT I LEARNED

WHAT DID I LEARN ABOUT JESUS

SOMETHING I AM GRATEFUL FOR

DRAW A PICTURE ABOUT TODAY'S LESSON

BIBLE STUDY NOTES

DATE _____

BOOK   CHAPTER   VERSES

WHO OR WHAT WAS THE LESSON ABOUT?

WHAT DOES THIS HAVE TO DO WITH ME?

A PICTURE OF WHAT I AM GRATEFUL FOR

WHAT HAPPENS?

BIBLE STUDY NOTES

DATE _____

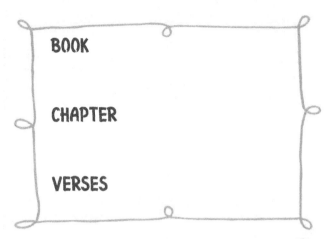

BOOK

CHAPTER

VERSES

TODAY I SANG

DRAW A PICTURE

TODAY I LEARNED

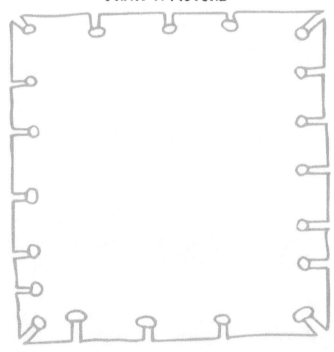

I FEEL GOD'S LOVE FOR ME...

I AM GRATEFUL FOR

_____

_____

AND IT MAKES ME FEEL

GOOD   GREAT   AWESOME

1.

2.

3.

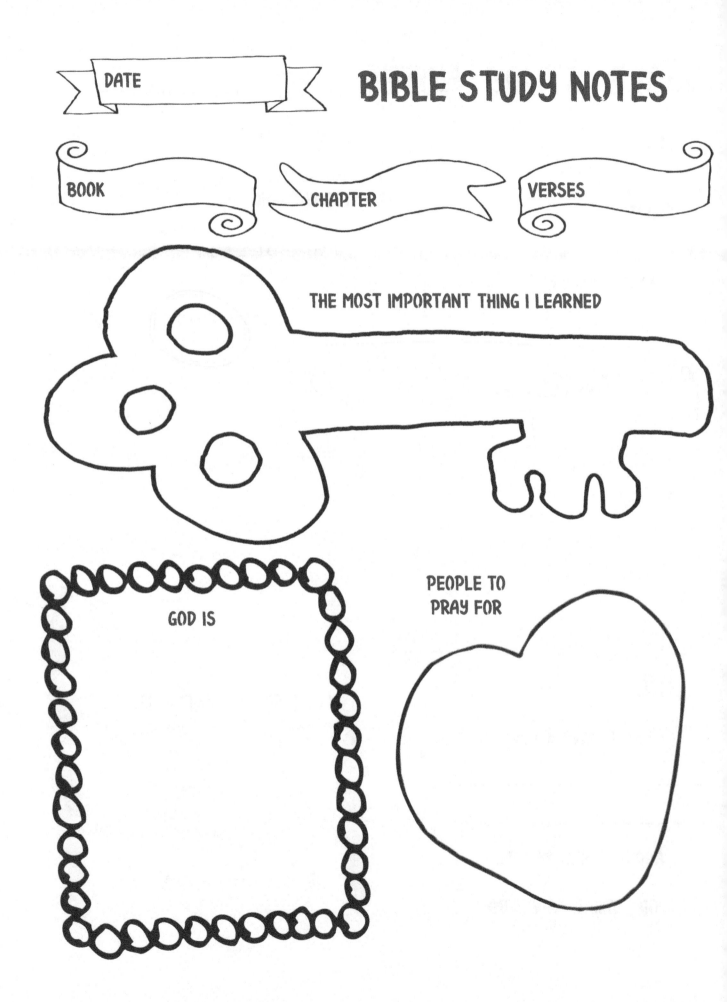

DATE

BIBLE STUDY NOTES

BOOK

CHAPTER

VERSES

THE MOST IMPORTANT THING I LEARNED

GOD IS

PEOPLE TO PRAY FOR

The following words can be found in the diagram below reading forward, backward, up, down and diagonally. Find the words and circle them.

altar   jacob
israel   priesthood
nativity   repent
atonement   flesh
mark   adam
wilderness   woman

```
Y A L T A R G I J A C O B Y W F
V S T M R P H F I G B K S V Y P
U K N A S L W P Z C L F Q B R S
Z I S R A E L Z P E U L H I Y M
X G R K F M T Q F P P E E A Z D
N T L Z I K C U B E M S A E C W
A F Z J E L H K D N T H X X D I
T D M S E A L V T H X X V W G L
I H Y A J D C N O N K H Q O R D
V Q G Z U A E O S H F V U M E E
I D T Y G M D F Q K R M I A P R
T O I O E W H P G K D Q R N E N
Y T H N X T B P A H L U K E N E
S R O K J B C W J Q F Y N M T S
N T T W Q K N K R L D T B D A S
A N Y L S R C C B D F Y N W D L
```

BIBLE STUDY NOTES

DATE _____

BOOK

CHAPTER

VERSES

SONGS WE SANG

THE MOST IMPORTANT THING I LEARNED

HOW CAN I USE WHAT I LEARNED

WHAT DID I LEARN ABOUT JESUS

SOMETHING I AM GRATEFUL FOR

DRAW A PICTURE ABOUT TODAY'S LESSON

BIBLE STUDY NOTES

DATE _____

BOOK   CHAPTER   VERSES

WHO OR WHAT WAS
THE LESSON ABOUT?

WHAT DOES THIS
HAVE TO DO WITH ME?

WHAT HAPPENS?

A PICTURE
OF WHAT I AM
GRATEFUL FOR

BIBLE STUDY NOTES

DATE _____

BOOK

CHAPTER

VERSES

TODAY I SANG

DRAW A PICTURE

TODAY I LEARNED

I AM GRATEFUL FOR

_____

AND IT MAKES ME FEEL

GOOD   GREAT   AWESOME

I FEEL GOD'S LOVE FOR ME...

1.

2.

3.

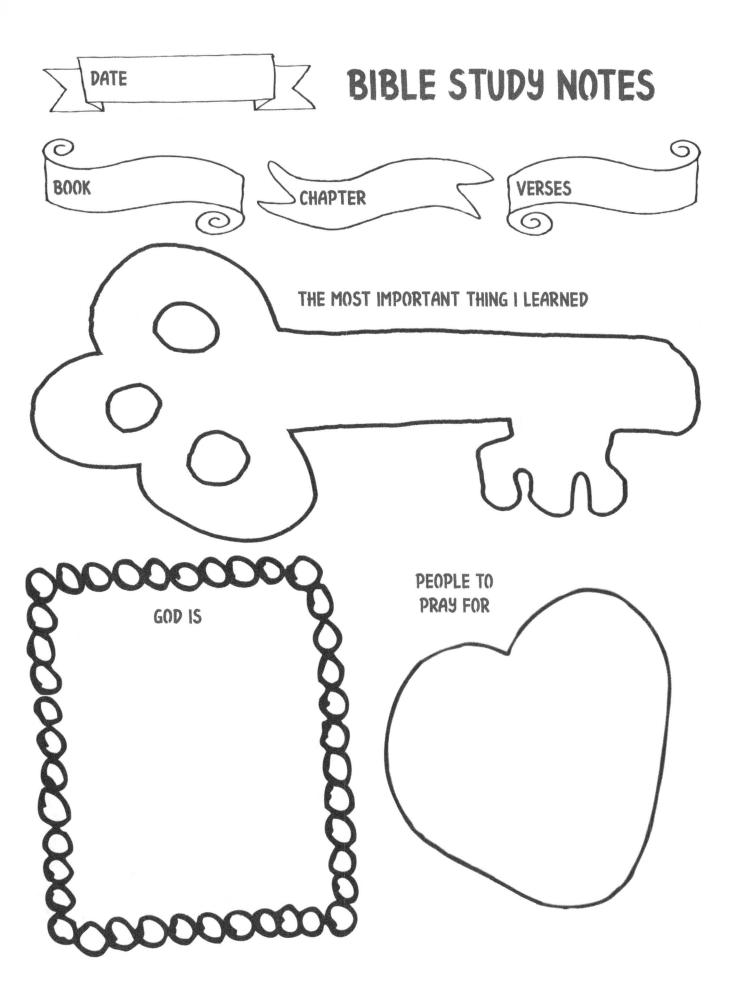

DATE

BIBLE STUDY NOTES

BOOK

CHAPTER

VERSES

THE MOST IMPORTANT THING I LEARNED

GOD IS

PEOPLE TO PRAY FOR

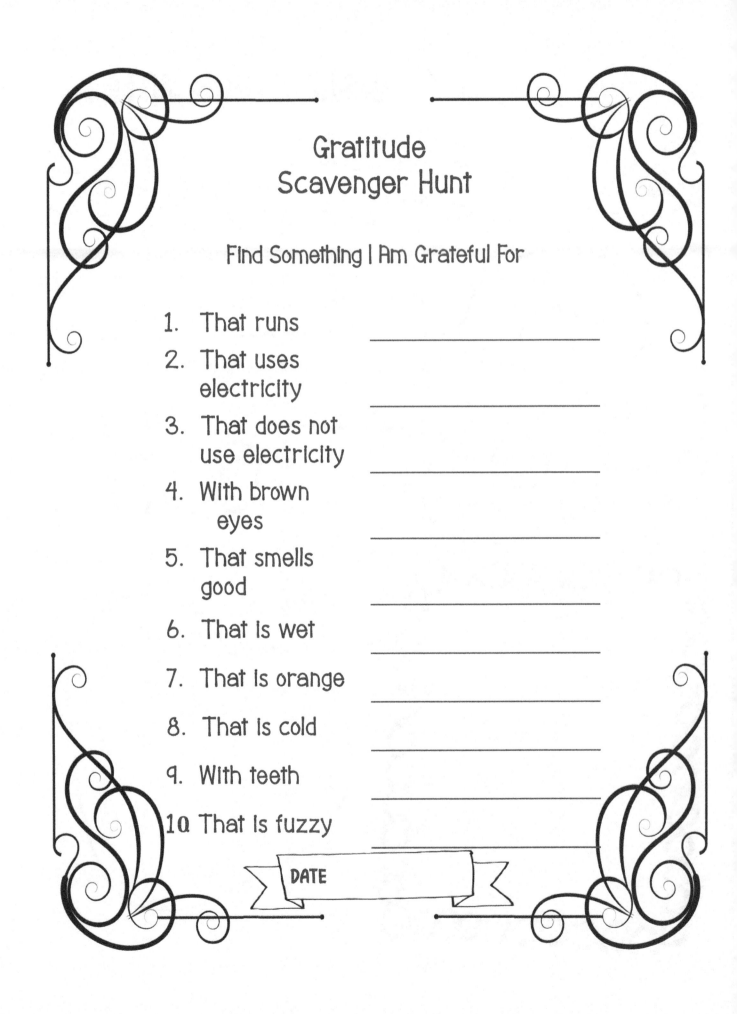

Gratitude Scavenger Hunt

Find Something I Am Grateful For

1. That runs _____

2. That uses electricity _____

3. That does not use electricity _____

4. With brown eyes _____

5. That smells good _____

6. That is wet _____

7. That is orange _____

8. That is cold _____

9. With teeth _____

10. That is fuzzy _____

DATE

BIBLE STUDY NOTES

DATE _____

BOOK

CHAPTER

VERSES

SONGS WE SANG

THE MOST IMPORTANT THING I LEARNED

HOW CAN I USE WHAT I LEARNED

WHAT DID I LEARN ABOUT JESUS

SOMETHING I AM GRATEFUL FOR

DRAW A PICTURE ABOUT TODAY'S LESSON

BIBLE STUDY NOTES

DATE _____

BOOK　　CHAPTER　　VERSES

WHO OR WHAT WAS
THE LESSON ABOUT?

WHAT DOES THIS
HAVE TO DO WITH ME?

A PICTURE
OF WHAT I AM
GRATEFUL FOR

WHAT HAPPENS?

BIBLE STUDY NOTES

DATE _____

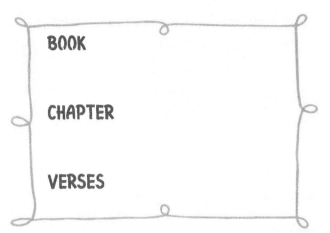

BOOK

CHAPTER

VERSES

TODAY I SANG

DRAW A PICTURE

TODAY I LEARNED

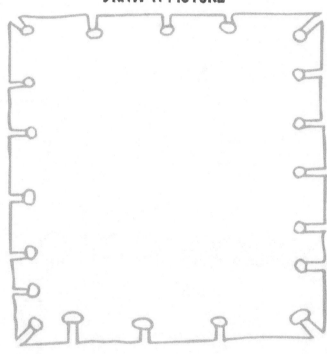

I FEEL GOD'S LOVE FOR ME...

1.

2.

3.

I AM GRATEFUL FOR

_____

_____

AND IT MAKES ME FEEL

GOOD   GREAT   AWESOME

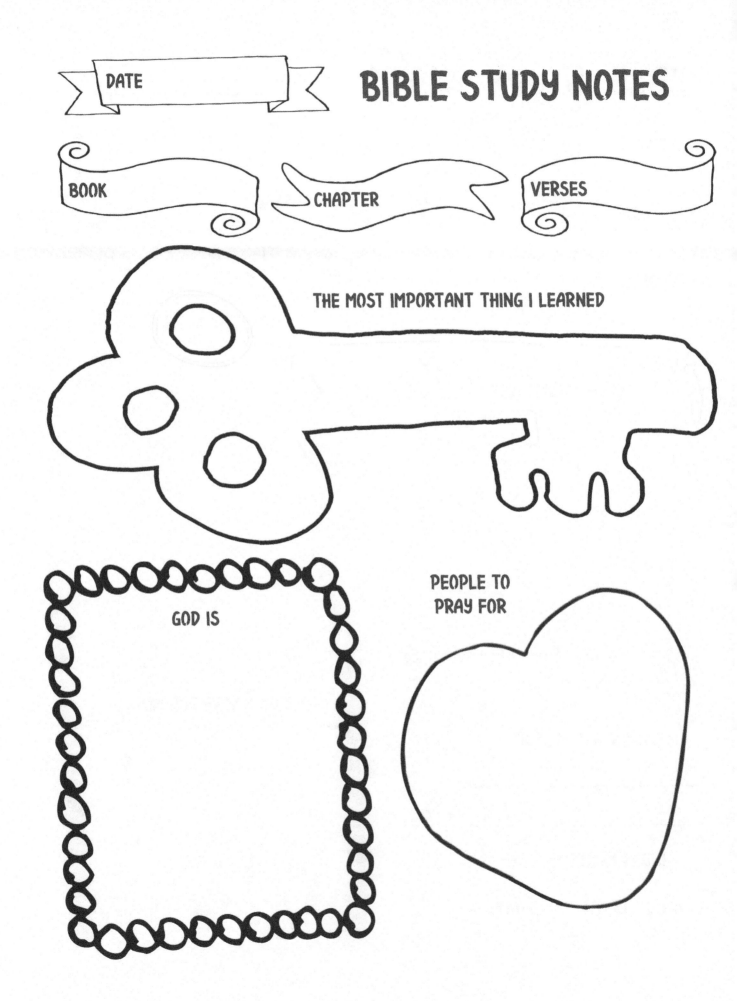

DATE

BIBLE STUDY NOTES

BOOK

CHAPTER

VERSES

THE MOST IMPORTANT THING I LEARNED

GOD IS

PEOPLE TO
PRAY FOR

Tell a favorite Bible Story as a Comic Strip

DATE:

BIBLE STUDY NOTES

DATE _____

BOOK

CHAPTER

VERSES

SONGS WE SANG

THE MOST IMPORTANT THING I LEARNED

HOW CAN I USE WHAT I LEARNED

WHAT DID I LEARN ABOUT JESUS

SOMETHING I AM GRATEFUL FOR

DRAW A PICTURE ABOUT TODAY'S LESSON

BIBLE STUDY NOTES

DATE _____

BOOK   CHAPTER   VERSES

WHO OR WHAT WAS
THE LESSON ABOUT?

_____
_____
_____
_____
_____
_____
_____

WHAT DOES THIS
HAVE TO DO WITH ME?

A PICTURE
OF WHAT I AM
GRATEFUL FOR

WHAT HAPPENS?

_____
_____
_____
_____
_____
_____

BIBLE STUDY NOTES

DATE _____

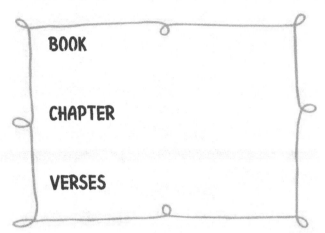

BOOK

CHAPTER

VERSES

TODAY I SANG

DRAW A PICTURE

TODAY I LEARNED

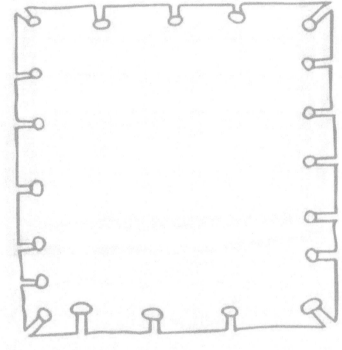

I AM GRATEFUL FOR

_____

_____

AND IT MAKES ME FEEL

GOOD   GREAT   AWESOME

I FEEL GOD'S LOVE FOR ME...

1.

2.

3.

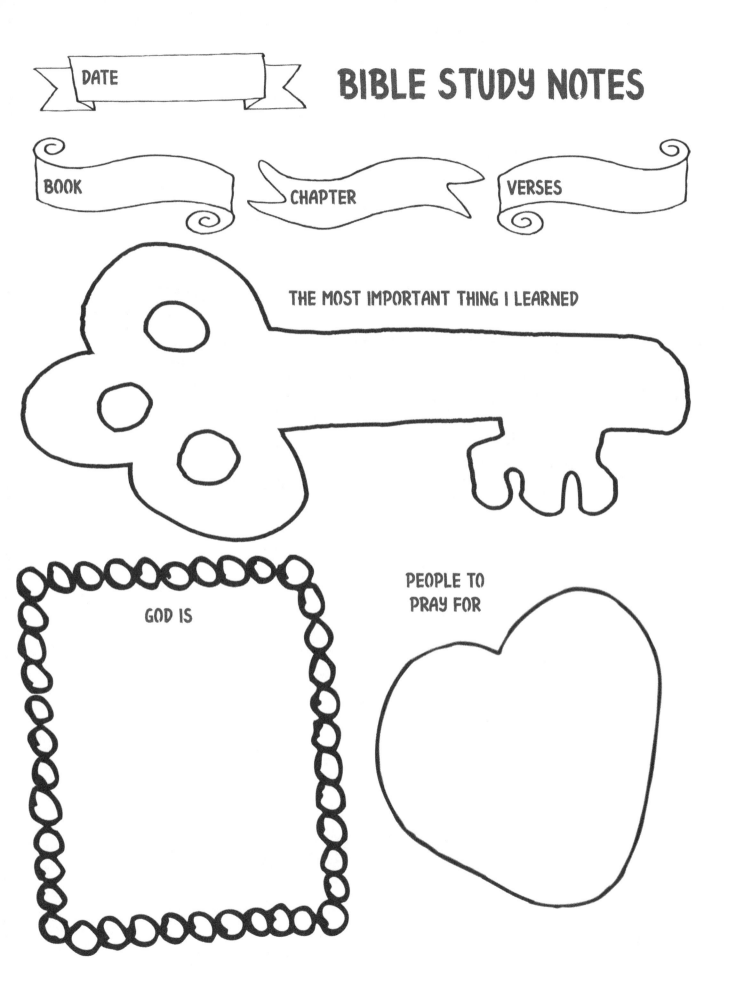

DATE

BIBLE STUDY NOTES

BOOK

CHAPTER

VERSES

THE MOST IMPORTANT THING I LEARNED

GOD IS

PEOPLE TO PRAY FOR

The following words can be found in the diagram below reading forward, backward, up, down and diagonally. Find the words and circle them.

exodus	testimony
disciple	temple
egypt	people
chapter	eve
mark	grace
genesis	jesus

```
S D W T E S T I M O N Y L Y M Q
M B I Z E V E E A Y K E B M G A
A Y X S G R A C E N K Z J W T N
R F F N C K G G G R E T I G S M
K G R X L I S J S T H P H S O Q
O H E E G Y P T U N R F T Y M K
D F S J X F Q L P C B I L T C T
J J M X A A F E E V T W A M V M
X Y R Q H P V X F Y Z N J T P D
C Y Q S Z Z Q F D S M Y A M L V
T Z I U T R Y B H U I Z M S Y Z
E C R D P G T O W J E S U S T N
M P E O P L E N Z Q Z X E R M I
P M M X R G D Q H K K H W N D F
L W F E W L L Q Z I K M V J E D
E U H C H A P T E R U H Q H T G
```

BIBLE STUDY NOTES

DATE _____

BOOK

CHAPTER

VERSES

SONGS WE SANG

THE MOST IMPORTANT THING I LEARNED

HOW CAN I USE WHAT I LEARNED

WHAT DID I LEARN ABOUT JESUS

SOMETHING I AM GRATEFUL FOR

DRAW A PICTURE ABOUT TODAY'S LESSON

BIBLE STUDY NOTES

DATE _____

BOOK   CHAPTER   VERSES

WHO OR WHAT WAS
THE LESSON ABOUT?

WHAT DOES THIS
HAVE TO DO WITH ME?

A PICTURE
OF WHAT I AM
GRATEFUL FOR

WHAT HAPPENS?

BIBLE STUDY NOTES

DATE _____

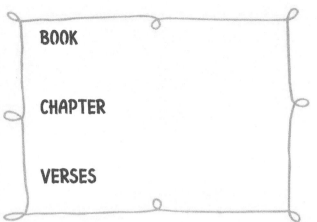

BOOK

CHAPTER

VERSES

TODAY I SANG

DRAW A PICTURE

TODAY I LEARNED

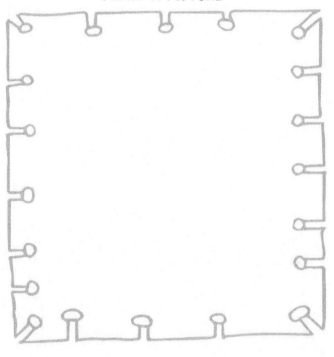

I FEEL GOD'S LOVE FOR ME...

1.

2.

3.

I AM GRATEFUL FOR

_____

_____

AND IT MAKES ME FEEL

GOOD   GREAT   AWESOME

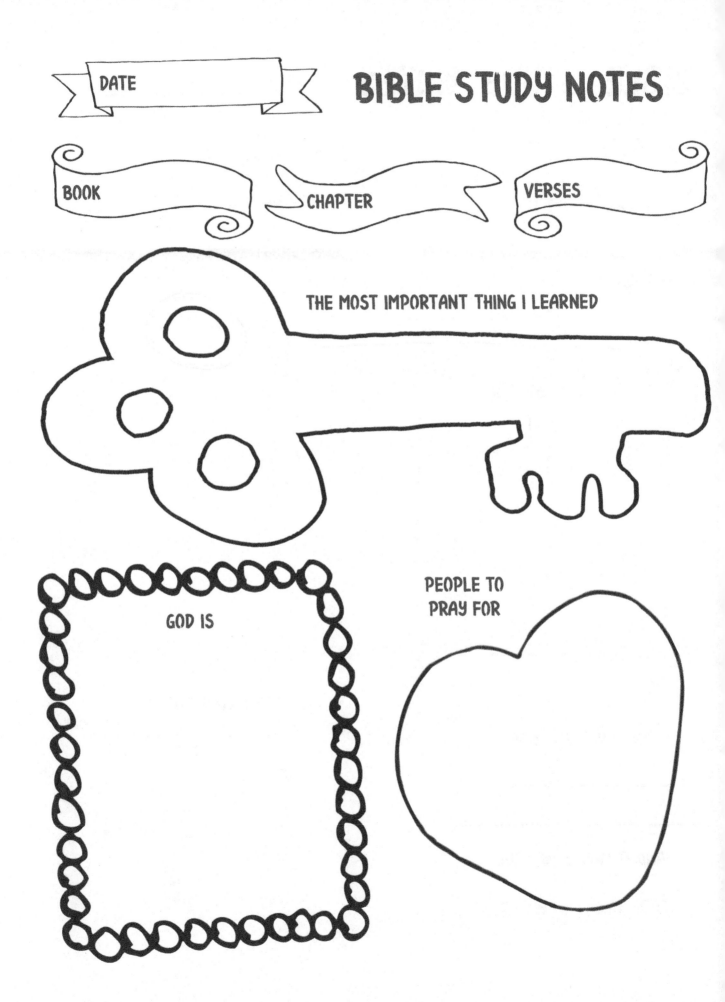

DATE

BIBLE STUDY NOTES

BOOK

CHAPTER

VERSES

THE MOST IMPORTANT THING I LEARNED

GOD IS

PEOPLE TO PRAY FOR

Gratitude
Scavenger Hunt

Find Something I Am Grateful For

1. That is green _____

2. That bends _____

3. With leaves _____

4. That jumps _____

5. That is made of wood _____

6. That moves with the wind _____

7. That smells bad _____

8. That is star shaped _____

9. That is funny _____

10 That is in nature _____

DATE

BIBLE STUDY NOTES

DATE _____

BOOK

CHAPTER

VERSES

SONGS WE SANG

THE MOST IMPORTANT THING I LEARNED

HOW CAN I USE WHAT I LEARNED

WHAT DID I LEARN ABOUT JESUS

SOMETHING I AM GRATEFUL FOR

DRAW A PICTURE ABOUT TODAY'S LESSON

BIBLE STUDY NOTES

DATE _____

BOOK   CHAPTER   VERSES

WHO OR WHAT WAS THE LESSON ABOUT?

WHAT DOES THIS HAVE TO DO WITH ME?

A PICTURE OF WHAT I AM GRATEFUL FOR

WHAT HAPPENS?

BIBLE STUDY NOTES

DATE _____

BOOK

CHAPTER

VERSES

TODAY I SANG

DRAW A PICTURE

TODAY I LEARNED

I FEEL GOD'S LOVE FOR ME...

1.

2.

3.

I AM GRATEFUL FOR

_____

_____

AND IT MAKES ME FEEL

GOOD   GREAT   AWESOME

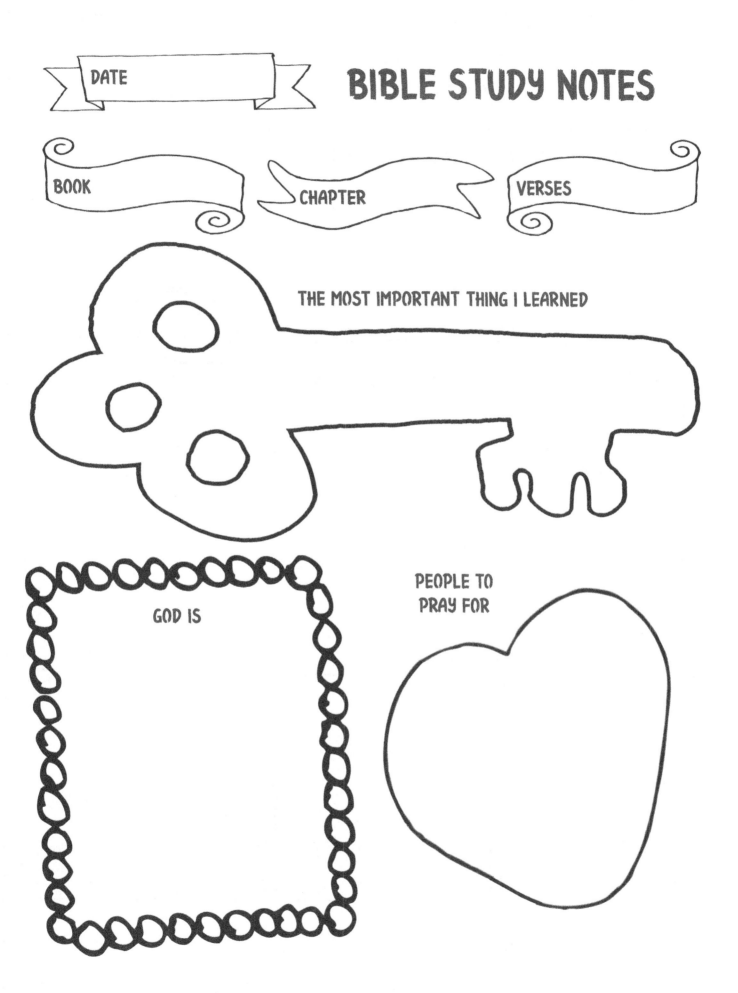

DATE

BIBLE STUDY NOTES

BOOK

CHAPTER

VERSES

THE MOST IMPORTANT THING I LEARNED

GOD IS

PEOPLE TO
PRAY FOR

Tell a favorite Bible Story as a Comic Strip

DATE:

BIBLE STUDY NOTES

DATE _____

BOOK

CHAPTER

VERSES

SONGS WE SANG

THE MOST IMPORTANT THING I LEARNED

HOW CAN I USE WHAT I LEARNED

WHAT DID I LEARN ABOUT JESUS

SOMETHING I AM GRATEFUL FOR

DRAW A PICTURE ABOUT TODAY'S LESSON

BIBLE STUDY NOTES

DATE _____

BOOK   CHAPTER   VERSES

WHO OR WHAT WAS
THE LESSON ABOUT?

_____
_____
_____
_____
_____
_____
_____
_____
_____

WHAT DOES THIS
HAVE TO DO WITH ME?

A PICTURE
OF WHAT I AM
GRATEFUL FOR

WHAT HAPPENS?

_____
_____
_____
_____
_____
_____
_____

BIBLE STUDY NOTES

DATE _____

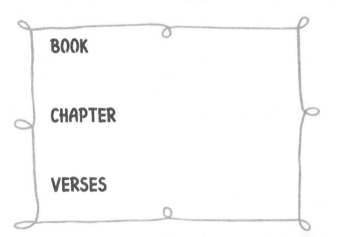

BOOK

CHAPTER

VERSES

TODAY I SANG

DRAW A PICTURE

TODAY I LEARNED

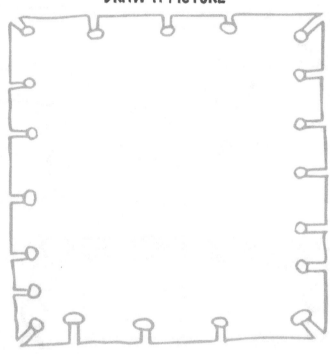

I FEEL GOD'S LOVE FOR ME...

1.

2.

3.

I AM GRATEFUL FOR

_____

_____

AND IT MAKES ME FEEL

GOOD   GREAT   AWESOME

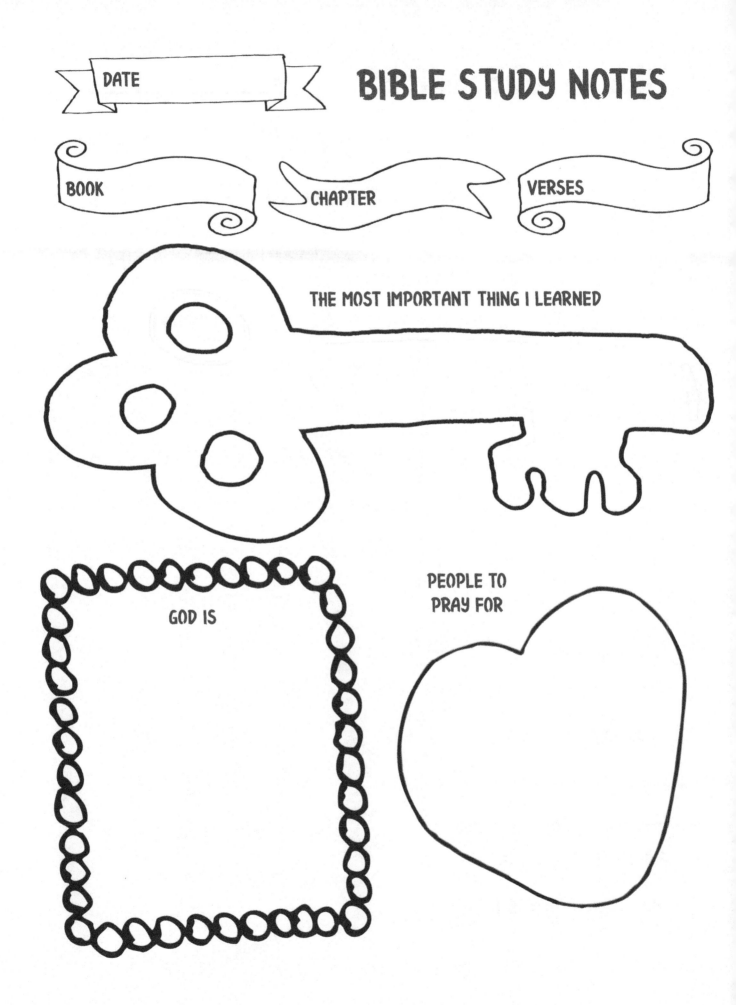

DATE

BIBLE STUDY NOTES

BOOK

CHAPTER

VERSES

THE MOST IMPORTANT THING I LEARNED

GOD IS

PEOPLE TO
PRAY FOR

The following words can be found in the diagram below reading forward, backward, up,
down and diagonally. Find the words and circle them.

jacob   paradise
luke   jesus
glory   silver
lucifer   mind
ishmael   christ
revelation   priest

```
O P Y S R E V E L A T I O N D Z
J Z A N J E S U S W J F E M A T
A A T R Z D F L S P R I E S T Q
C B Z A A E Q R S V N G U G J T
O F M I N D X Q P C V C D P C W
B O G C A Z I T C Z T G Q K Y M
Y F G E P A J S M Q Y P M A S B
D P P K S Q J L E S J E Z Z P X
L N C R R S R B E I A U U A N V
G E C L R O V B Y L G U H L U G
L A R S E N U L U K E J F M B G
O R J G V L E H Z Z L A C K A X
R M Z D L H H O B N P T M G C O
Y C H R I S T P H B Q N S H A U
E E B D S D N F O O C B N G S J
U V L I L U C I F E R K E O N I
```

BIBLE STUDY NOTES

DATE _____

BOOK

CHAPTER

VERSES

SONGS WE SANG

THE MOST IMPORTANT THING I LEARNED

HOW CAN I USE WHAT I LEARNED

WHAT DID I LEARN ABOUT JESUS

SOMETHING I AM GRATEFUL FOR

DRAW A PICTURE ABOUT TODAY'S LESSON

BIBLE STUDY NOTES

DATE _____

BOOK   CHAPTER   VERSES

WHO OR WHAT WAS
THE LESSON ABOUT?

WHAT DOES THIS
HAVE TO DO WITH ME?

WHAT HAPPENS?

A PICTURE
OF WHAT I AM
GRATEFUL FOR

BIBLE STUDY NOTES

DATE _____

BOOK

CHAPTER

VERSES

TODAY I SANG

DRAW A PICTURE

TODAY I LEARNED

I FEEL GOD'S LOVE FOR ME...

I AM GRATEFUL FOR

_____

_____

AND IT MAKES ME FEEL

GOOD   GREAT   AWESOME

1.

2.

3.

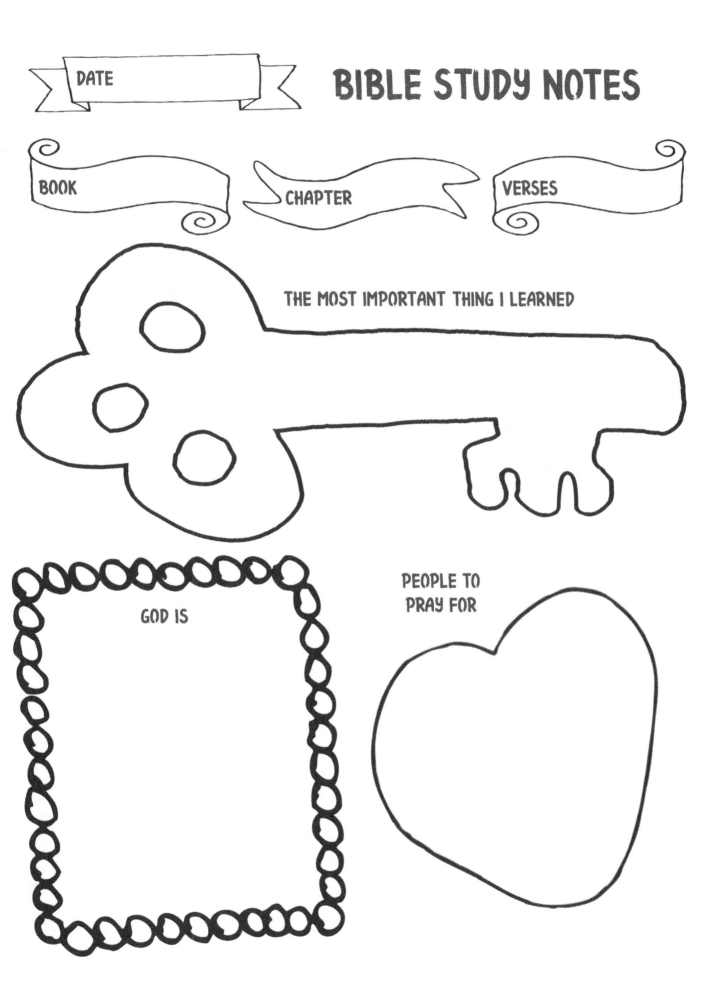

DATE

BIBLE STUDY NOTES

BOOK

CHAPTER

VERSES

THE MOST IMPORTANT THING I LEARNED

GOD IS

PEOPLE TO PRAY FOR

Gratitude
Scavenger Hunt

Find Something I Am Grateful For

1. That floats _____
2. That sparkles _____
3. That is a rectangle _____
4. That hops _____
5. That is wavy _____
6. That flies _____
7. That is hot _____
8. That grows _____
9. That is pink _____
10. That is colorful _____

DATE

BIBLE STUDY NOTES

DATE _____

BOOK

CHAPTER

VERSES

SONGS WE SANG

THE MOST IMPORTANT THING I LEARNED

HOW CAN I USE WHAT I LEARNED

WHAT DID I LEARN ABOUT JESUS

SOMETHING I AM GRATEFUL FOR

DRAW A PICTURE ABOUT TODAY'S LESSON

BIBLE STUDY NOTES

DATE _____

BOOK   CHAPTER   VERSES

WHO OR WHAT WAS
THE LESSON ABOUT?

WHAT DOES THIS
HAVE TO DO WITH ME?

A PICTURE
OF WHAT I AM
GRATEFUL FOR

WHAT HAPPENS?

BIBLE STUDY NOTES

DATE _____

BOOK

CHAPTER

VERSES

TODAY I SANG

DRAW A PICTURE

TODAY I LEARNED

I FEEL GOD'S LOVE FOR ME...

I AM GRATEFUL FOR

_____

_____

1.

2.

3.

AND IT MAKES ME FEEL

GOOD   GREAT   AWESOME

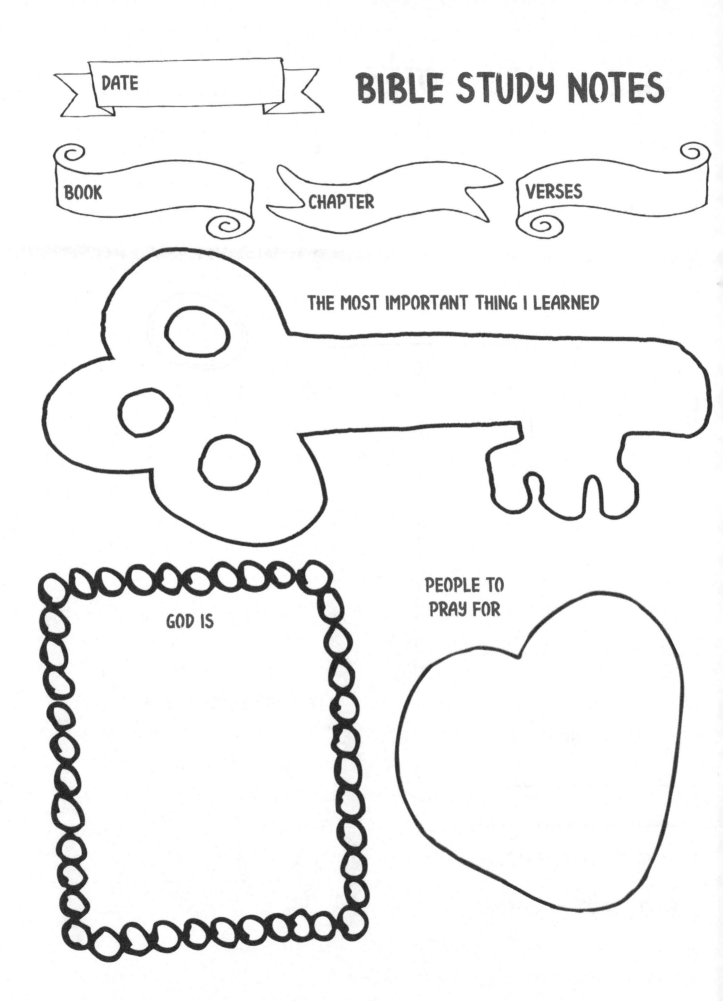

DATE

BIBLE STUDY NOTES

BOOK

CHAPTER

VERSES

THE MOST IMPORTANT THING I LEARNED

GOD IS

PEOPLE TO PRAY FOR

Tell a favorite Bible Story as a Comic Strip

DATE:

BIBLE STUDY NOTES

DATE _____

BOOK

CHAPTER

VERSES

SONGS WE SANG

THE MOST IMPORTANT THING I LEARNED

HOW CAN I USE WHAT I LEARNED

WHAT DID I LEARN
ABOUT JESUS

SOMETHING I AM GRATEFUL FOR

DRAW A PICTURE ABOUT TODAY'S LESSON

BIBLE STUDY NOTES

DATE _____

BOOK   CHAPTER   VERSES

WHO OR WHAT WAS
THE LESSON ABOUT?

WHAT DOES THIS
HAVE TO DO WITH ME?

WHAT HAPPENS?

A PICTURE
OF WHAT I AM
GRATEFUL FOR

BIBLE STUDY NOTES

DATE _____

BOOK

CHAPTER

VERSES

TODAY I SANG

DRAW A PICTURE

TODAY I LEARNED

I FEEL GOD'S LOVE FOR ME...

1.

2.

3.

I AM GRATEFUL FOR

_____

AND IT MAKES ME FEEL

GOOD   GREAT   AWESOME

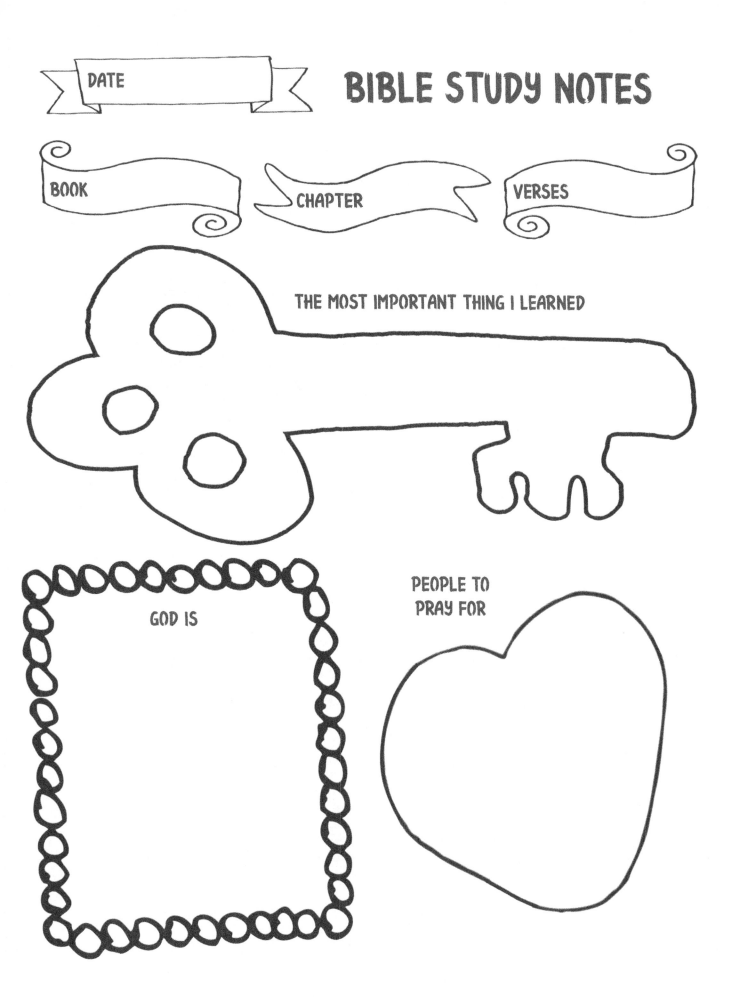

DATE

BIBLE STUDY NOTES

BOOK

CHAPTER

VERSES

THE MOST IMPORTANT THING I LEARNED

GOD IS

PEOPLE TO PRAY FOR

The following words can be found in the diagram below reading forward, backward, up, down and diagonally. Find the words and circle them.

patriarch	saul
cain	jehovah
bread	holy
prodigal	bethlehem
glory	temple
david	heart

```
C A I N T D G D W T S A U L C B
D N B U G R S D S M U P O R T B
X I R G F Q I C P D W T K Z E Q
P T E M P L E E C R H P L T O P
R H A E S Z Q M O E E G H I C A
O M D P H C Y K R C G L L M F T
D B Q I S Y X E N E E O J G D R
I A S S F W B H J H R R P L P I
G Z D R F O D L E P U Y T H I A
A T R N D G H M W W M A W E H R
L F T B A A C U J L L Y X A O C
B X A S V D P W P F Q J N R L H
K B A O I R X X E Y U J R T Y V
M M H F D X X D V Z B W R F L N
V E Q E E D O G E F D C J C W T
J T S F F X D D B Y C C U U I G
```

BIBLE STUDY NOTES

DATE _____

BOOK

CHAPTER

VERSES

SONGS WE SANG

THE MOST IMPORTANT THING I LEARNED

HOW CAN I USE WHAT I LEARNED

WHAT DID I LEARN ABOUT JESUS

SOMETHING I AM GRATEFUL FOR

DRAW A PICTURE ABOUT TODAY'S LESSON

BIBLE STUDY NOTES

DATE _____

BOOK   CHAPTER   VERSES

WHO OR WHAT WAS
THE LESSON ABOUT?

WHAT DOES THIS
HAVE TO DO WITH ME?

A PICTURE
OF WHAT I AM
GRATEFUL FOR

WHAT HAPPENS?

BIBLE STUDY NOTES

DATE _____

BOOK

CHAPTER

VERSES

TODAY I SANG

DRAW A PICTURE

TODAY I LEARNED

I FEEL GOD'S LOVE FOR ME...

1.

2.

3.

I AM GRATEFUL FOR

_____

_____

AND IT MAKES ME FEEL

GOOD   GREAT   AWESOME

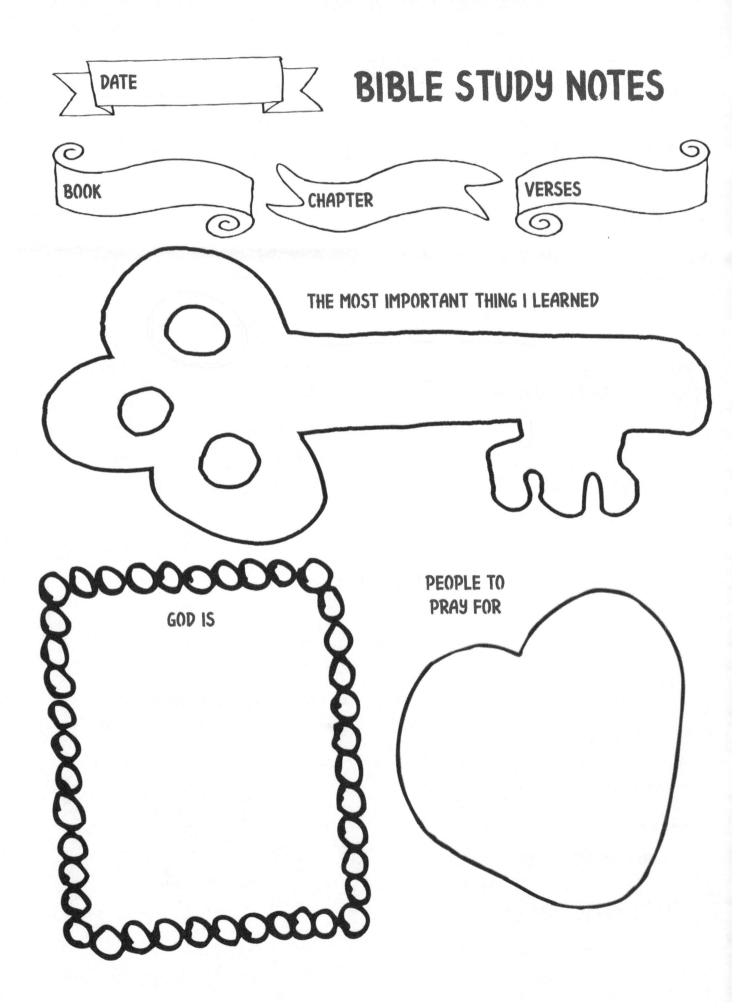

DATE

BIBLE STUDY NOTES

BOOK

CHAPTER

VERSES

THE MOST IMPORTANT THING I LEARNED

GOD IS

PEOPLE TO PRAY FOR

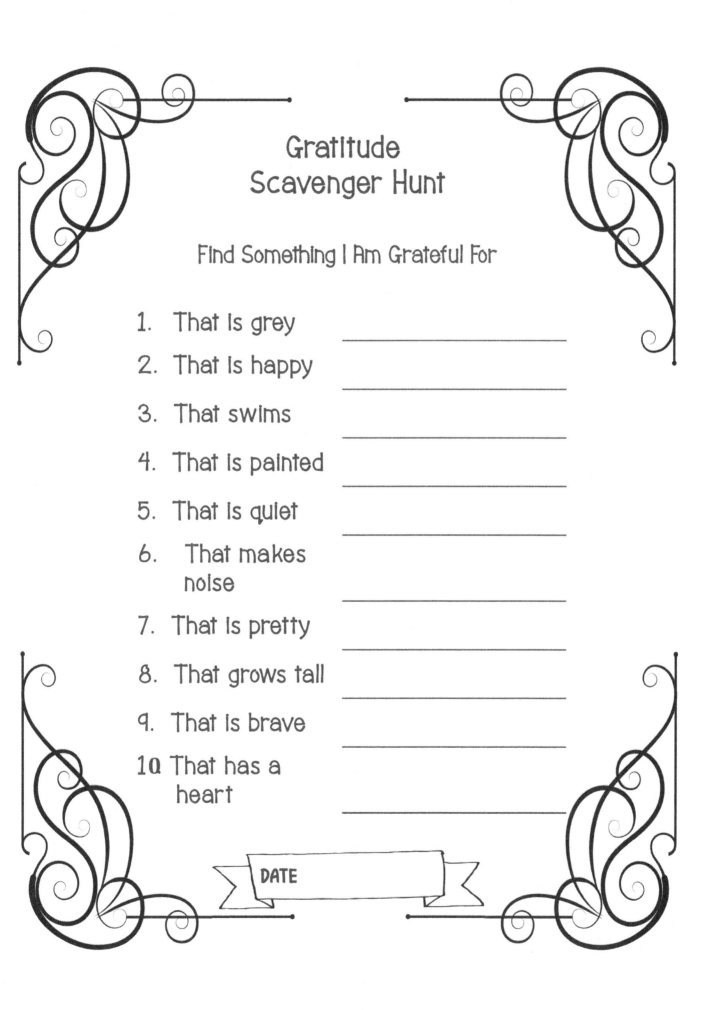

Gratitude
Scavenger Hunt

Find Something I Am Grateful For

1. That is grey _____

2. That is happy _____

3. That swims _____

4. That is painted _____

5. That is quiet _____

6. That makes noise _____

7. That is pretty _____

8. That grows tall _____

9. That is brave _____

10 That has a heart _____

DATE

BIBLE STUDY NOTES

DATE _____

BOOK

CHAPTER

VERSES

SONGS WE SANG

THE MOST IMPORTANT THING I LEARNED

HOW CAN I USE WHAT I LEARNED

WHAT DID I LEARN ABOUT JESUS

SOMETHING I AM GRATEFUL FOR

DRAW A PICTURE ABOUT TODAY'S LESSON

BIBLE STUDY NOTES

DATE _____

BOOK   CHAPTER   VERSES

WHO OR WHAT WAS THE LESSON ABOUT?

WHAT DOES THIS HAVE TO DO WITH ME?

WHAT HAPPENS?

A PICTURE OF WHAT I AM GRATEFUL FOR

BIBLE STUDY NOTES

DATE _____

BOOK

CHAPTER

VERSES

TODAY I SANG

DRAW A PICTURE

TODAY I LEARNED

I FEEL GOD'S LOVE FOR ME...

I AM GRATEFUL FOR

_____

_____

AND IT MAKES ME FEEL

GOOD   GREAT   AWESOME

1.

2.

3.

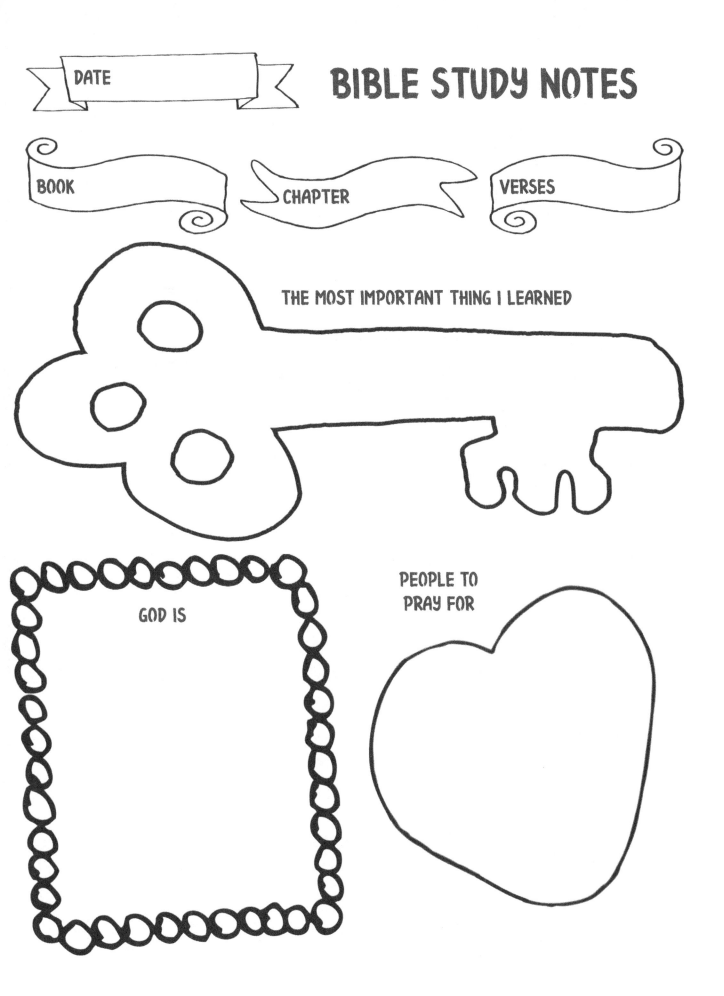

DATE

BIBLE STUDY NOTES

BOOK

CHAPTER

VERSES

THE MOST IMPORTANT THING I LEARNED

GOD IS

PEOPLE TO PRAY FOR

Tell a favorite Bible Story as a Comic Strip

DATE:

BIBLE STUDY NOTES

DATE _____

BOOK

CHAPTER

VERSES

SONGS WE SANG

THE MOST IMPORTANT THING I LEARNED

HOW CAN I USE WHAT I LEARNED

WHAT DID I LEARN ABOUT JESUS

SOMETHING I AM GRATEFUL FOR

DRAW A PICTURE ABOUT TODAY'S LESSON

BIBLE STUDY NOTES

DATE _____

BOOK   CHAPTER   VERSES

WHO OR WHAT WAS
THE LESSON ABOUT?

WHAT DOES THIS
HAVE TO DO WITH ME?

WHAT HAPPENS?

A PICTURE
OF WHAT I AM
GRATEFUL FOR

BIBLE STUDY NOTES

DATE _____

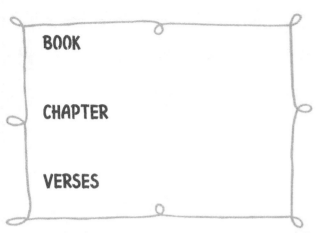

BOOK

CHAPTER

VERSES

TODAY I SANG

DRAW A PICTURE

TODAY I LEARNED

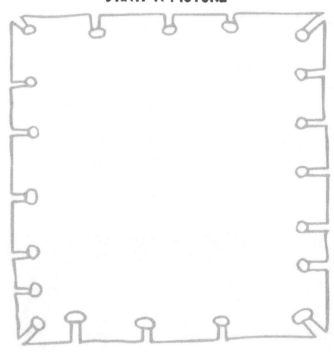

I AM GRATEFUL FOR

_____

_____

AND IT MAKES ME FEEL

GOOD   GREAT   AWESOME

I FEEL GOD'S LOVE FOR ME...

1.

2.

3.

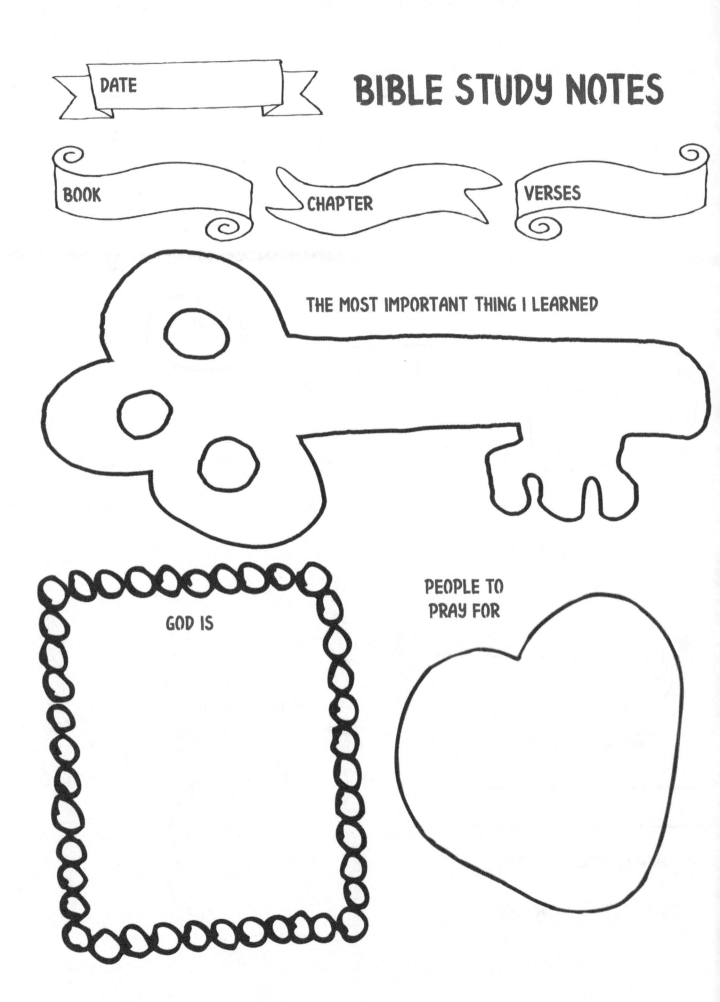

DATE

BIBLE STUDY NOTES

BOOK

CHAPTER

VERSES

THE MOST IMPORTANT THING I LEARNED

GOD IS

PEOPLE TO
PRAY FOR

The following words can be found in the diagram below reading forward, backward, up, down and diagonally.   Find the words and circle them.

eve	john
love	blood
holy	sacrifice
baptism	nations
brother	verses
mark	power

```
N Q R D O A J R E H T O R B V E
R A O Z Y P K R N X Q X E V W V
Y Y T E G M E K F W P O W E R E
P P N I G S B H B X Z P W R X F
G P S L O V E E F Q J C P S H G
W U L G Z N I W O V C H X E K I
U J Y Q H E S W W X B C O S K E
D R L Z L X G L F C Z B E H Y P
B Q S Z O I G T F D Q G F E Q K
L I I W I T T O M E Y Q E A V L
O Y K B R J Q Z Q S J F T A M H
O Z E D J N L F V F I Z J K Y O
D Z O Y U A W F C N P T S N F L
C T J O H N Z C G Z H K P I U Y
W O Q B N M A R K Z L L Y A A J
T A G Y D E C I F I R C A S B U
```

BIBLE STUDY NOTES

DATE _____

BOOK

CHAPTER

VERSES

SONGS WE SANG

THE MOST IMPORTANT THING I LEARNED

HOW CAN I USE WHAT I LEARNED

WHAT DID I LEARN ABOUT JESUS

SOMETHING I AM GRATEFUL FOR

DRAW A PICTURE ABOUT TODAY'S LESSON

BIBLE STUDY NOTES

DATE _____

BOOK   CHAPTER   VERSES

WHO OR WHAT WAS
THE LESSON ABOUT?

_____
_____
_____
_____
_____
_____
_____

WHAT DOES THIS
HAVE TO DO WITH ME?

A PICTURE
OF WHAT I AM
GRATEFUL FOR

WHAT HAPPENS?

_____
_____
_____
_____
_____
_____
_____

BIBLE STUDY NOTES

DATE _____

BOOK

CHAPTER

VERSES

TODAY I SANG

DRAW A PICTURE

TODAY I LEARNED

I FEEL GOD'S LOVE FOR ME...

1.

2.

3.

I AM GRATEFUL FOR

_____

_____

AND IT MAKES ME FEEL

GOOD   GREAT   AWESOME

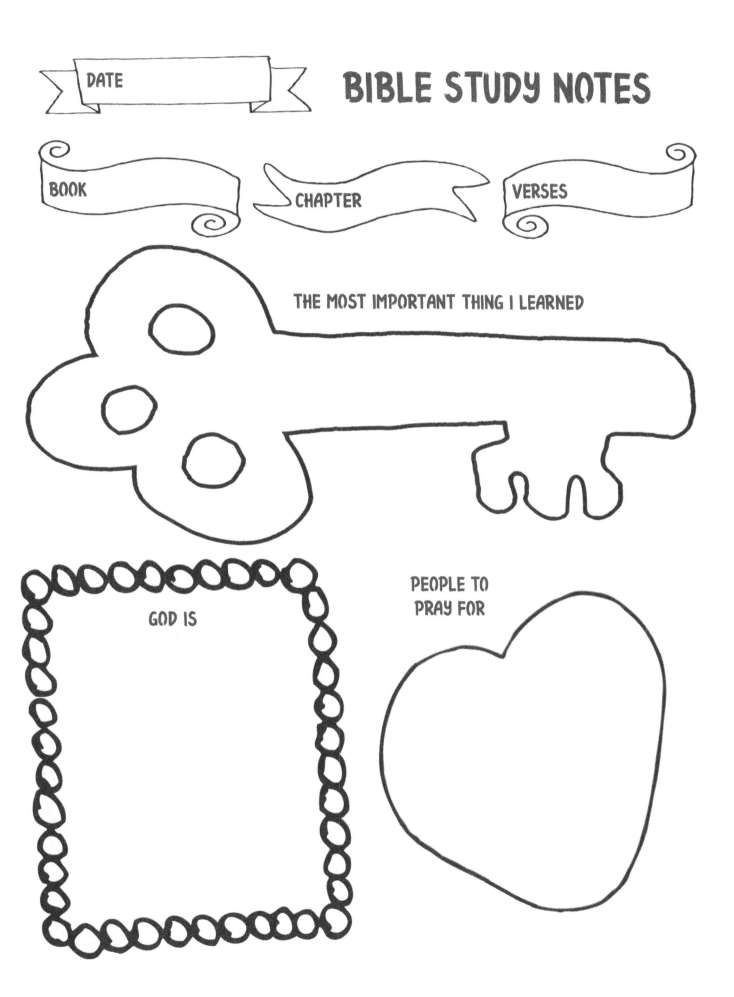

DATE

BIBLE STUDY NOTES

BOOK

CHAPTER

VERSES

THE MOST IMPORTANT THING I LEARNED

GOD IS

PEOPLE TO PRAY FOR

Gratitude
Scavenger Hunt

Find Something I Am Grateful For

1. That is purple _____

2. That is crazy _____

3. That has fingers _____

4. That sleeps
   during the day _____

5. That tastes
   sweet _____

6. That lights up _____

7. That is dark _____

8. That is a food _____

9. That is liquid _____

10 That is loud _____

DATE

BIBLE STUDY NOTES

DATE _____

BOOK

CHAPTER

VERSES

SONGS WE SANG

THE MOST IMPORTANT THING I LEARNED

HOW CAN I USE WHAT I LEARNED

WHAT DID I LEARN ABOUT JESUS

SOMETHING I AM GRATEFUL FOR

DRAW A PICTURE ABOUT TODAY'S LESSON

BIBLE STUDY NOTES

DATE _____

BOOK   CHAPTER   VERSES

WHO OR WHAT WAS
THE LESSON ABOUT?

WHAT DOES THIS
HAVE TO DO WITH ME?

WHAT HAPPENS?

A PICTURE
OF WHAT I AM
GRATEFUL FOR

BIBLE STUDY NOTES

DATE _____

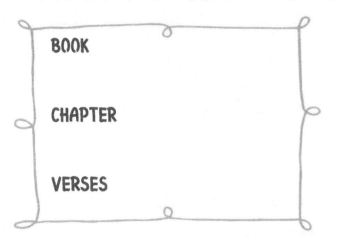

BOOK

CHAPTER

VERSES

TODAY I SANG

DRAW A PICTURE

TODAY I LEARNED

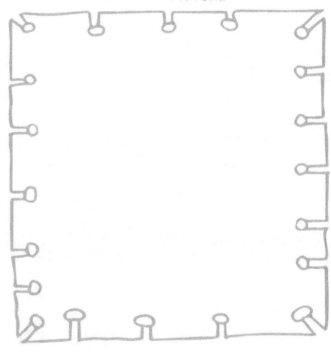

I FEEL GOD'S LOVE FOR ME...

1.

2.

3.

I AM GRATEFUL FOR

_____

_____

AND IT MAKES ME FEEL

GOOD   GREAT   AWESOME

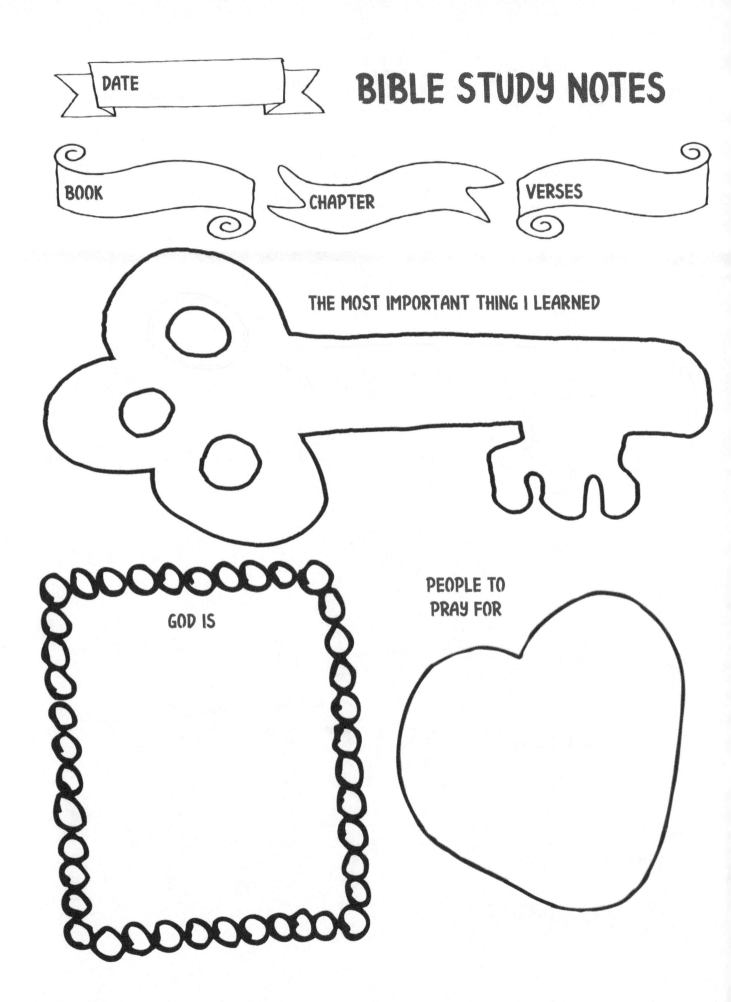

DATE

BIBLE STUDY NOTES

BOOK

CHAPTER

VERSES

THE MOST IMPORTANT THING I LEARNED

GOD IS

PEOPLE TO
PRAY FOR

Tell a favorite Bible Story as a Comic Strip

DATE:

The following words can be found in the diagram below reading forward, backward, up, down and diagonally. Find the words and circle them.

repentance	moses
eve	exodus
glory	cain
bread	jerusalem
grace	rapture
tabernacle	soul

```
E T Y R E P E N T A N C E R F N
V F A L Q K G R A C E X K O K E
E I A B I E C A I N G C D U N F
P U J A E V H L G G C L U H X K
S U G L O R Y V G E Z P F H U L
K X G Y D V N S M V O U G U B J
F V R D G J X A B Q C A G H I A
T T Y Z R C V J C O R X J X R K
H X G Y A M H Y O L Y B O E I X
E C S Q D C H F X E E R U O O D
B M U G O T E U R F R H Z D V X
R E D K C N H H Q S O U L Y K S
E M O S E S F Q P X K E T L O Q
A S X C K W X B B F B F A P Z K
D L E B X T J N R U F X K V A U
U Z G J E R U S A L E M I Q Y R
```

26973021R00057